Four Essays on Karma

by
Yuen Liao Fan

Translated by
Evelyn Li & K.C. Ng

Revised and edited by
Acharya Kender Tomko

Purple Lotus Society
San Bruno, California, U.S.A.

Four Essays on Karma

First Edition

Library of Congress Cataloging-in-Publication Data
Yüan, Liao-fan, 1533-1606.
 [Liao-fan ssu hsün. English]
 Four Essays on Karma / Yuen Liao Fan ; translated by Evelyn Li
 & K.C. Ng ; revised and edited by Acharya Kender Tomko. —
 1st ed.
 p. cm.
 ISBN 1-881493-02-4 (pbk.) : $5.00
 1. Ethics, Chinese. I. Li, Evelyn. II. Ng, K.C. (Kwok C), 1957- .
 III. Tomko, Acharya Kender. IV. Title.
 BJ117.Y813 1995
 181'.043--dc20   95-5210
                                                          CIP

Printed in the United States of America

Contents

Acknowledgments 5

A Brief Biography of the Author 6

Introduction 7

Essay I. How to Determine One's Destiny

1.1   The Course of Life Is Prearranged 13

1.2   One Creates One's Own Karma 15

1.3   Heavenly Calamities Can Be Averted 17

1.4   Those Ignorant of Magic Charms Will Be
       Ridiculed by the Spirits and Heavenly Beings ... 19

1.5   Worthy Persons Content with Their Fate 21

1.6   The Modest Person Attains Tao 23

Essay II. Methods of Self-Correction

2.1   Three Essentials of Self-Correction 24

2.2   The Three Levels of Correction 27

Essay III. The Ways of Accumulating Merit

3.1   Meritorious Families Have Blessings From
       Generation to Generation 30

3.2 Everyone Can Be Compassionate 32

3.3 Heaven Has Compassion 33

3.4 Inner Guidance Inspires Continued Public
Service 35

3.5 Freeing Innocent Convicts Brings the Blessing
of Heaven 37

3.6 Respecting and Protecting the Buddha Way
Brings Prosperity 38

3.7 Different Kinds of Virtue 40

3.8 Authentic and Inauthentic Virtue 41

3.9 Superficial and Courageous Virtue 42

3.10 Open and Hidden Virtue 43

3.11 The Influence of Long-term and Short-term
Virtue 44

3.12 The Consequences of Responsible and
Complacent Virtue 46

3.13 Thoroughness of Virtue Depends on
Sincerity 47

3.14 The Degree of Merit Depends on
Scope of Intent 49

3.15 Ten Different Ways to Exercise Virtue 51

Essay IV. Humility

4.1 The Value of Humility 57

Acknowledgments

The Purple Lotus Society would like to thank the following persons for making this translation possible:

Grand Master Sheng-yen Lu (Living Buddha Lian-sheng) for His blessing and guidance; Master Lian-hsiang and Master Samantha Chou for their encouragement; Evelyn Li for initiating this project and providing the first draft of translation; Janny Chow and Kwok C. Ng for revising the translated manuscript; Pamela Ziv Johnson for English editing; Kender Tomko for final editing and revision; Shirley Hsiao and Kevin Henderson for desktop publishing; and Ellen Hsu for the cover design.

A Brief Biography of the Author

Mr. Yuen Liao Fan, originally named Yuen Huang, was born during the Ming Dynasty in 1533 A.D. in the Kiangsu Province of mainland China.

He was a renowned scholar in his time who made a deep study of such fields as astrology, the humanities (including music), mathematics, and physics. Yuen wrote numerous books and earned great respect as a high government official. He died at the age of 74, about five years after writing this volume.

Introduction

Tuan-mu Tzu inquired, "Is there any single word which will keep us on the correct path till the end?"
Master Kung-fu Tze responded, "Yes there is: reciprocity. What you do not wish for yourselves, do not inflict upon others." — Analects of Confucius —

This volume is a translation of a centuries old Chinese book on "karma," which means causality, the relationship between cause and effect in life. Karma is a Hindu-Buddhist term with many levels of meaning. In essence, karma refers both to people's conscious actions in life, and to what befalls them in life. The fundamental theme underlying this book is to demonstrate reciprocity between intention and outcome, primarily on the personal level. The purpose is simply to serve as a "book of examples," by which people may identify and train in the development of higher levels of virtue.

The incentive is classically Buddhist: time and again, charitable acts are seemingly rewarded with more favorable life circumstances. Typical examples in this book are the success in a government qualifying examination, where the individual had previously failed, and the birth of a child to a couple who had been childless. Please note that in a Confucian social order, such as is found in this book, government examination results largely determine social status, and offspring largely determine family wealth.

In modern Western thinking, opportunities and benefits are more likely the result of other factors. *Four Essays on Karma* attempts to demystify and elucidate the "workings of karma" to help people better understand life, therefore becoming both more noble and more effective in their daily lives.

In principle, this book should be accessible to all high school students and young adults. It would, in fact, be of great value in Asian and multi-cultural studies programs, due to the clear and effective way it presents a classical Chinese Buddhist view of life. Similarly, this book would be of profound value to anyone who wishes to engage in Asian spiritual culture. As a book of traditional Chinese wisdom it needs some cultural introduction, at least for modern Westerners who, by world historical standards, are significantly mono-cultural, ahistorical, and individualistic.

By these measures Chinese culture is also absolutely mono-cultural, subject to ages-long historical inertia, and completely organized on the basis of the extended family. Indeed, one of the names which Chinese have for their homeland is "The Ancient Hundred Family Names." This alone speaks volumes about Chinese culture and history.

A brief perspective on traditional Chinese culture is appropriate. It must be kept in mind however that Chinese culture is essentially contextual in nature and, hence, not simply explained in Western terms. Just as traditional Chinese bioenergetic medicine can never be dissected in terms of Western physical medicine, it is impossible to even partially interpret Chinese spiritual life in terms of conventional Western religion. Attempting to do so would only obscure or prevent real understanding. Modern society, being multi-cultural, cannot afford this.

Westerners sincerely interested in understanding the "Chinese way of life" can only proceed by incorporating some significant part of it into their own lives. For example, one can practice Tai Chi, use Chinese medicine, or examine and work with life in the light of this text. The Westerner who can really engage one or more of the classical Chinese inner disciplines is someone who has gone a long way towards transcending the materialistic limitations of Western culture and developing their own inner nature.

The essence of human life is relationship. Every breath and every movement we make is in relationship, of relationship, by relationship, and through relationship. In all the principal Asian systems of social organization and spiritual culture (Hinduism, Buddhism, Confucianism, and Taoism) relationship is held to be primary, although in markedly different ways. Classical China was home to three of these major systems: the Confucian, the Taoist, and the Buddhist. This is clearly reflected throughout these Essays, where the Confucian ethic, Taoist practices, and Mahayana Buddhist principles are thoroughly integrated, as they were in practice in the Middle Kingdom for over a thousand years.

Classical Chinese views on "conscious human relationships" are the subject of this book, specifically from the standpoint of what the Chinese call "teh," which means virtue or spirit. For example, the title of a principal Taoist book, the *Tao Teh Ching*, has been translated as "The Way of Life and Its Virtue," but this could also be translated as "The Spirit of the Natural Way of Human Development."

Buddhists, Taoists, and Confucians may individually or collectively disagree on particulars of "teh," but all agree that the conscious development of "virtuous spirit" is vital both to the individual and to society. *Four Essays on Karma* was written to address just this topic, and it has remained for several centuries a popular and highly regarded "book of virtues" among traditional Chinese. Perhaps by sharing this translation with their English-speaking children, Asian and Buddhist parents can preserve more of the cultural continuity so necessary for inter-generational understanding.

Balance and natural harmony are central to the Chinese view of life, regardless of which of the three systems is emphasized. A Confucian focuses on developing community well-being through responsible social organization, thus balanced and harmonious human relations are essential. A Taoist seeks natural realization through union with the forces of nature, thus balance and harmony with nature is emphasized. A Chinese Buddhist focuses on the liberation of inner human potential through transcendent awareness, thus the balanced and harmonious expression of the inner Buddha-nature is paramount.

In all three systems, however, virtue is understood to be developed through conscious integration of the individual with the "greater whole." The traditional Chinese image of "Heaven, Earth and Humanity" places human life and consciousness between the physical Earth and the transcendent Heaven.

This perspective recognizes the simultaneous importance of both material and transcendent being, and therefore the need to "walk in balance" between them, whether as a Buddhist, Taoist, or Confucian. All people face the same issues, regardless of how we label ourselves in spiritual terms.

As humans we speak of developing personal maturity, of going forward in life. The author of "The Little Prince," Antoine de Saint-Expéry, once said, "The individual is a path. Only he [or she] matters who takes the path." To consciously take a life path requires one to clarify, assess, and prioritize one's own intentions. This is a major focus of the present volume. The teachings and examples given in this book can be of tremendous benefit to us. They contain the wisdom of long ago and far away, offering — as though from a mountain — a much broader and higher perspective on basic human issues.

Transcending the modern belief in a separate, fixed, and anxious self is essential to this path of "walking in balance." For example, the Chinese character (word-picture) for "tao," or way of life, is based on the image of a person walking down a road. Here, the sense of journey is primary, while the subjective sense of "person" and the objective sense of "road" are also necessary aspects of the overall picture.

Those who have travelled widely know that travelling reveals much about oneself and about humanity in general. It is both deeply personal and remarkably universal. This is exactly the feeling of tao, of personal revelation and development along the road of life. It is not a frantic search outside oneself for something to grasp onto. Traditional spiritual practitioners are quieter, more thoughtful and deliberate and, in particular, more disciplined in consciousness.

We choose life pathways (through our thoughts and actions). These pathways respond in kind and begin choosing us. The conscious sense of personal journey interacts with the circumstances of life, producing a personal tao within the overall tao of life. This is the real reason for accepting and practicing the inner disciplines. By purifying and strengthening our thoughts and actions, we clarify and stabilize our lives. This becomes of ever greater importance as society begins to unravel, and circumstances become less stable and less reliable.

There is tremendous historical precedent for this. Through six thousand years of recorded history, the Chinese have repeatedly undergone chaos and catastrophe. Many imperial regimes have come and gone, yet the inner spiritual culture of the Chinese people has remained alive and well. The strength of the Chinese has always derived from their strong sense of family ties, their emphasis on education for social advancement, and their strong inner spiritual life.

Traditional wisdom and spiritual practice emphasize that one's individual character development is one's destiny. However, nothing in modern culture encourages inner development; inner development is entirely ignored. However, we as individuals are not prevented from developing social support networks, from educating ourselves, or from practicing yoga and developing inner spiritual life. Even in modern society we are as free to succeed in life as we are free to fail.

Therefore, this translation is dedicated to you, the reader, in the hope that you will be inspired to go forward in your own life. Ideally, you will become an individual who inspires those around you to go forward in their own lives. In that case, you will have truly realized your human birthright.

Those who wish to develop a deeper, more personal, and more active involvement with classical Chinese Buddhist spiritual work should realize that it is truly possible to accomplish this, even in modern America. This translation, for example, is published under the auspices of the Purple Lotus Society, the San Francisco branch of the True Buddha School, a Chinese Buddhist-Taoist fellowship.

In the last ten years, formal membership in this Tantric [esoteric spiritual] fellowship has grown from eighty thousand members to over two million members. Of this number, at least one million are presently active, mostly throughout the Pacific Rim. There are fifteen chapters in North America, and others are being organized in Europe. I point this out because it demonstrates the perseverance and universal nature of inner wisdom culture as expressed in this book. Despite the fact that Buddhist Asia has been brutally crushed in this century under militarism, nationalism, and Communism, Buddhist culture is being reborn as World Buddhism. In particular, expatriate Chinese Buddhists are keeping alive their traditional wisdom culture. This is happening throughout the world, far from its original home. To borrow from John Cage, they are unlike the snail because they carry their homes within them! And so can we all.

May all beings benefit!

Acharya Kender Tomko
September 1994

Essay I. How to Determine One's Destiny

1.1 The Course of Life Is Prearranged

I lost my father while still a child. My mother felt that the medical profession would be best for me since it would benefit others and provide a good livelihood. Such had also been my father's hope. I therefore gave up all thought of taking the civil service examinations.

One day at Mercy Cloud Monastery, I came across a pious elder with the physical appearance of an immortal. He said to me, "Young man, you are destined to be a government official[1]. You will be a county administrator next year. Why then aren't you studying?"

I explained to him my reasons, and humbly asked his name and origin. He said, "I am of the Kung family from Yunan. I have been given Shao Tzu's *Huang Chi Shu [The Supreme Method of Fortune Telling]*, and you are destined to inherit it." At this, I invited him to become my house guest.

Once home I related this encounter to my mother, who advised me to treat him with utmost respect. Again and again, she tested his fortune-telling abilities and to our amazement, his accuracy was beyond all doubt. Hence, I followed his advice to study in preparation for a county administrative post.

Mr. Kung then started to "read" my destiny. "On your first Imperial exam," he said, "you will rank fourteenth. On your second exam, you will rank seventy-second. And on your third exam, you will rank ninth." That year I passed all three exams, just as predicted by Mr. Kung. To my great surprise, I placed exactly as he had predicted! I was totally intrigued by these events and requested of him a complete reading for the rest of my life.

---

[1]During this time in China, government officials were held in very high esteem.

He then analyzed my future, predicting when I would pass the civil service exam, when I would be a county junior officer, and when I would be promoted to be a senior administrator. Eventually, I would become a county magistrate. Then three and a half years later, he said, I would retire. Finally, I would die childless at age fifty-three on the fourteenth of the eighth lunar month, between the hours of one and three a.m.

As time passed, every one of my exam scores were those infallibly predicted by Mr. Kung, regardless of my diligence.

When I was junior official, Mr. Kung foretold that I would be promoted to a senior position when my allowance of government rice accumulated to 91.5 hectoliters (2420 gallons). After I had 70 hectoliters (1850 gallons), my supervisor recommended me for promotion and so I began to doubt Mr. Kung's prediction. But this endorsement was rejected. The following year, I was given another such recommendation and this time successfully promoted. I then counted the rice I got and it totalled exactly 91.5 hectoliters!

From then on I was convinced that life was an expression of fate. And as a result I lost all ambition, aspiration, and desire.

1.2 One Creates One's Own Karma

As time passed, I was sent to the capital to study for a year. Instead of studying, I spent most of my time in meditation.

Upon returning to Nanking, I journeyed to Chi Hsia Mountain to visit Zen Master "Cloud Valley." We practiced Zen meditation together for three days and nights without rest.

Master Cloud Valley then said, "You have meditated for three days and nights without interfering thoughts or desires, unlike commoners. May I ask the reason for this?"

I replied, "A Mr. Kung has convinced me that my life is predetermined. There is no reason for any presumptuous thoughts or desires."

Master Cloud Valley responded, "A person who does not awaken their inner nature and bring forth pure awareness[2] will be entirely subject to the push and pull of the Cosmos, and hence have no freedom. However, the truly compassionate are not fettered by inherited karma and neither are the truly wicked. So for these twenty years, you have let yourself be conditioned by karma! You are just an ordinary being while I thought you were a sage." He then burst into laughter.

At this I asked, "So, are you saying that personal fate can be changed?"

"Yes," the Master responded. "A proverb says: '*A person's life is determined from within, and one's outer appearance is projected from the mind. Calamity and good fortune never enter except when invited.*' Furthermore, a Buddhist scripture says: '*One shall have good fortune, longevity, or a son or daughter as one asks.*' This is not just worthless talk. Absence of guile is a fundamental Buddhist teaching, and the Buddhas and Bodhisattvas[3] do not deceive."

---

[2]Pure awareness transcends all categories of "higher" or "lower," "inner" or "outer," "temporary" or "permanent," "before" or "after." In it, all thoughts and experience rise and fall within one encompassing mindfulness like the waves upon the vast ocean.

[3]Bodhisattva means one who is committed to ultimate realization in order to benefit all living beings.

"But Mencius advised people to aspire only towards that which can be cultivated, such as loyalty and a upright character. Prestige and wealth however come from others. How can one cultivate these?" I asked.

"Mencius speaks the truth, but you need to understand further. The sixth Zen patriarch Hui-neng said, 'All seeds of fortune arise within one's mind. Seek within your own heart to fulfill your hopes.' The individual should seek help from within, and strive assiduously towards goodness. Through earning the respect of society the outer good fortune of prosperity, fame and success will naturally follow. If a person doesn't seek within his [or her] heart, then all pursuits of fame and wealth, no matter how strenuous, will be in vain."

1.3 Heavenly Calamities Can Be Averted

Master Cloud Valley then asked, "How did Mr. Kung foretell your future?"

I told him the entire story without hesitation.

"Do you feel you deserve to be a top official, and to have a son?" he asked.

I reflected for a while, and then replied, "The faces of most high officials indicate virtue while I am poor in virtue. I have not performed enough charity. I am impatient, intolerant, conceited, and insensitive. I give in to passion, and speak heedlessly. All of these indicate lack of virtue so I must not deserve a top government post.

"As the proverb says, 'river sediments nourish many creatures, while pure waters carry no fish.' I am fastidious to a fault, and that makes me non-social, a reason to expect no male heir. Life flourishes in harmonious conditions, but my temper is hot and stormy, and this is a second reason to expect no male heir. Compassion is important when raising children, but I am too selfish for empathy and self-sacrifice: that's a third reason to deserve no male heir. There are many other reasons: I waste my energy by speaking too much; I dissipate myself in drink; I carelessly stay up all night, and so on .... These are all good reasons for having no male heir."

Master Cloud Valley responded, "There are many more missed opportunities in life than career and family! There are karmic principles by which each of us falls into this or that category, whether we are wealthy, extremely wealthy, or impoverished. Heaven simply facilitates the course of life by providing opportunities and guidance. As with the body, much depends on diet and physical constitution.

"Family history is also a matter of reaping what has been sown. Those who have many descendents must have accomplished much virtue.

"The point is that by understanding our own faults, we can correct them and thus change our karma. For example, we can transform greed into generosity, anger into love, hypocrisy into sincerity, sloth into diligence, and pride into humility. Start accumulating merit! Be kind, agreeable and tolerant towards others, and preserve your life energy. Drop the past and begin your life today, like a newborn child!

"Just as the physical body is governed by actions, so is the emotional body attuned to deliberate behavior. A spiritually renewed person is definitely blessed. There is a saying in the Book of History: 'Heavenly Calamities can be averted; but there is no way to escape the calamities people bring down upon themselves.' The Book of Odes states that 'Through understanding the harmonious way of life and through self-cultivation good fortune will come.'

"Mr. Kung described one possible future in which you would not be a top official and would have no child, but these are 'Heavenly Calamities' and can be averted. If you continuously sow a good crop of beneficial activities then you will always harvest good fortune.

"The Book of Changes was written to instruct the intelligent in how to follow the good and to avoid error, but if karma were fixed, then there would be no choice of paths. The first chapter of the Book of Changes says: 'A family of great virtue has good fortune from generation to generation.' Do you have faith in this?"

1.4 Those Ignorant of Magic Charms Will Be Ridiculed by the Spirits and Heavenly Beings

Suddenly I came to a new understanding; on receiving Master Cloud Valley's words I offered him reverence and then presented myself to the Buddhas, repenting all my past transgressions. I prayed for promotion and vowed to perform three thousand charitable acts in gratitude for the generosity of my ancestors, and the support of Heaven.

Master Cloud Valley instructed me to keep a [karmic] diary, and to balance out each transgression with a good deed. He then taught me to chant the Cundi[4] recitation to obtain empowerment in the fulfilment of my wish.

He said further that: "People who draw the magic charms[5] say, 'Those ignorant of magic charms will be ridiculed by the Spirits and Heavenly Beings.' The key to esoteric calligraphy is freedom from conceptual elaboration. First empty the mind and release all worldly concerns. In this pure awareness, paint the first point which represents the source of all existence. Then complete the calligraphy in one continuous movement so that it will embody spiritual power. Similarly, to supplicate Heaven, one must start with pure awareness.

"Mencius said, 'There is no difference between a life that is long and one that is short. Inner cultivation is the essential point.' Since everyone feels that length of life is most important, why did Mencius say this?

"Consider it this way: if one abides peacefully, free of grasping, hope, and fear, satisfied with whatever comes and fulfilling one's obligations, then what difference does it make? In fact, all relative distinctions such as those between "rich" and "poor", "noble" and "inferior" exist only in the mind. It is

---

[4]Cundi: an esoteric female divinity known to the Buddhists as Diamond Female Yogin and to the Hindus as Kali.

[5]Magical talismans: strips of paper inscribed with symbolic drawings which have magical power for cure and protection.

by indulging in vain hopes that people fail to face reality. They easily become excited or downcast, unable to meet good fortune and calamity with a balanced mind. To them, a "long" life and a "short" life are very different, but the key events in both are the same: birth and death. Our life is transient, however long or short. We should simply flow with events as they arise, whether difficult or fortunate.

"As for inner cultivation, correct mistakes and bring forth virtue. Be calm and focused in adversity. A person able to rest in equanimity with clear perception is very close to *awakening* [one's inner nature]. At that time, all obscurations dissolve, and karmic appearances arise simply as reflections of inner awareness, neither good nor bad.

"One who has not brought forth clear awareness can recite the Cundi formula continuously until awareness becomes transparent and open. In this state, one is not even conscious of the flow of recitation, which is in a sense comparable to the single continuous movement used for inscribing magic charms."

I then took the spiritual name *Liao Fan*, which means "Renouncing worldly affairs".

1.5 Worthy Persons Content with Their Fate

From that time on I began paying attention to my behavior. I used to be aimless and dissolute, but became cautious and conscientious, even when alone. Eventually I became able to shrug off the verbal harassments and calumnies of others.

The following year, I took another civil exam in which Mr. Kung predicted I would rank third, yet I ranked first. And that fall, I passed the preliminary exam to become eligible for provincial level imperial examinations, although this was completely unanticipated by Mr. Kung.

However, deeper reflection showed my inner cultivation to be inadequate. For example, doing half-hearted charity, helping others with hesitation, or giving a hand while speaking thoughtlessly. When sober I behaved, but became a bit wild when drunk. In this way many good deeds were cancelled by errors, and thus it took over ten years to accomplish the pledged three thousand good deeds. Upon visiting my home village the following year I was finally able to dedicate those deeds before the Buddhas. I then prayed for a son and vowed to enact another three thousand good deeds. One year later my wife gave birth to a son.

Each good deed I performed (whether feeding the poor, assisting others or freeing small animals) was recorded. My wife, being unlettered, would simply draw a circle on the calendar date. At times we were able to accomplish more than ten good deeds daily and so in a little over two years time, I accomplished the pledged three thousand. I quickly returned home and performed the dedication of merit, this time for success in the highest imperial examinations. I vowed to accomplish ten thousand good deeds.

Three years passed, and I attained the rank of district governor. I put a notebook on my desk and each day I would record all my deeds, whether good or bad, big or small. Each night I would pray to the Jade Emperor.

Seeing that I made little progress in charity, my wife said in concern, "When we lived a village life we accomplished three thousand good deeds in a rather short time. But in this government office, I can be of no help. How then can we accomplish ten thousand good deeds?"

Then one night I dreamt of a heavenly being and spoke to him about the difficulty of fulfilling the vow. He responded, "If you were to reduce the tax on farmer's produce, that would fulfill the vow."

The current grain tax rate of my district was very high at 23.7 per cent. I immediately mandated a reduction to 14.6 per cent. However, I doubted whether that one act could really equal ten thousand good deeds.

Fortuitously, a Zen master came from Five Platforms Mountain and I shared this dream and good deed with him. He then said, "Any charitable act carried out with a sincere heart is as good as ten thousand, especially a district-wide reduction of the grain tax! Thousands of people will benefit from this new law." Hearing that, I donated my salary to the Zen master to provide his monastery with food to complete my vow, and to thank Heaven for fulfilling my aspiration.

Mr. Kung had foretold that my life would not extend beyond 53 years. Although I had not prayed for longer life I lived through that year peacefully. I am now sixty nine years old.

As it is said in the Book of History: "Faith in Heaven is difficult, and there is no permanence in life." It also said: "Karma is not fixed." All these words are true.

As I now understand matters, those who claim that life is predetermined are superficial in their consciousness while those who see that life is determined from within the individual are wise.

1.6 The Modest Person Attains Tao

One cannot predict the course of events in their totality. Therefore, when one reaches a peak in life, prepare for a fall. When experiencing good fortune, be ready for adversity. Be prepared to be poor when one is enjoying great wealth. Expect slander when praised. Treat your family line, however honorable, as low birth. Always regard yourself as lacking knowledge even when well educated.

Praise the virtue of your ancestors, and remedy the faults of your parents. Repay the generosity of the country. Work for the benefit of coming generations. Help all those who are in great need, and shun both idleness and improper thought.

Try to reflect upon and correct mistakes daily. By failing to examine faults for even a single day, one falls back.

There are plenty of sharp people in this world. Few however are successful, simply because they do not cultivate their character. Settling for ease and comfort, they waste their precious human birth[6].

Master Cloud Valley's teaching on karma reveals the essential principle and constitutes the most profound truth, the flawless wisdom.

One should always recall this teaching to avoid squandering life.

---

[6]Precious human birth: Refers to the freedoms and qualities of a truly worthwhile existence, including health, freedom, and access to the Buddhist teachings.

Essay II. Methods of Self-Correction

2.1 Three Essentials of Self-Correction

During the Spring and Autumn Period [770-476 B.C.E.], many scholar-officials were able to predict the rise and fall of a person by weighing their words and actions. All were very accurate as demonstrated by examples in the Tso Chuan[1], and other histories of this period.

In general, signs of coming prosperity and misfortune originate within the heart, and manifest through one's demeanor. One who appears "thick" [stable, kind and generous], will usually encounter prosperity. On the other hand one who appears "thin" [unstable, flippant and untrustworthy], is prone to misfortune. It is only through lack of knowledge that people are unable to predict changes in personal fortune.

A person's kindness or lack thereof is known to Heaven. When an individual is to receive good fortune from above, this first becomes apparent through their composed and serene demeanor. And when someone is about to experience misfortune, this is also evident in their immature and irresponsible behavior. Those who seek to avoid misfortune and gain prosperity should first endeavor to correct past mistakes and only then take up charitable work. In this way individuals will be naturally guided towards virtue by the course of life itself.

The first essential point of self-correction is deep remorse. Just think of the heroes and heroines of past ages. How were they able to leave behind great legends? And why are the rest of us completely unknown, sometimes even left without family or resources?

Hungering only for status and wealth, engaging in surreptitious misconduct, brazen before others, one is even worse

---

[1]A commentary on the Spring and Autumn Annals.

than an animal. Nothing could be so shameful. As Mencius states, "Remorse has a great influence on man. Keeping it, one rises to become a sage, and losing it, one lowers oneself to the level of animals." Thus, heart-felt repentance is the gist of correction.

The second essential point is maintaining gravity and respect. Spirits and heavenly beings cannot be deceived. Even seemingly inconsequential wrongdoing is nevertheless recorded and judged by Heaven. We will [eventually] be punished according to the severity of the sum total of our transgressions.

One should therefore develop an attitude of gravity and respect towards heavenly beings. No matter where we might be, even when hidden in a sealed cave, we remain subject to their observation. The resonance of our thought patterns is heard by the spirits and heavenly beings. Because of this we must always respect them, whether or not we sense their presence.

Even when transgressions have piled up into the sky, an individual can still begin anew, given only that he or she yet breathes. History provides numerous examples of those who engaged only negativity until arriving at death's door, and yet died at peace due to a change of heart. This can be likened to the lamp which when lit banishes an eon-long darkness. Thus, it is never too late.

Life is impermanent and the physical body, since it is born as a confluence of karmic factors, must fall apart when those energies are exhausted. It is when the breath stops that one can no longer change personal karma, even in the spirit. Then severely distorted action carries on from lifetime to lifetime, and as a result the individual's distorted consciousness experiences a seemingly endless hell[2] of its own making, which even the Awakened Ones cannot purify. How can one not trem-

---

[2]Buddhist psychology describes eighteen kinds of hells, some hot, some cold, depending on the suffering deliberately caused others. Such a hell may seem to last many eons, but even so remains a "karmic vision" which dissolves when the causal factors are exhausted.

ble at this?

The third essential point of self-correction is courageous determination. It is due to hesitation that one fails to mend one's ways. Unwavering commitment is required to extract the thorns of small mistakes, and for cutting off the finger poisoned by a grave mistake. Free of any doubt one must strike like lightning, and then success is assured.

The person who possesses these three essential points will gradually become free of error, just as the winter's ice melts before the sun in springtime.

2.2 The Three Levels of Correction

There are three progressively deeper levels of transforming personal karma: (1) action, (2) analysis, and (3) pure awareness. Each is demonstrated differently and has a different result.

Correction at the level of action: One who in the past would kill or throw a fit refrains from doing so again. This however serves only to cut off manifest wrongdoing; it does not bring about inner purification.

Correction at the level of analysis: Murderous intent for example can be pacified by empathy. Since every living being cares deeply about its own kind, how can one be so callous as to boil or fry living beings just for a meal? Try to imagine the agony of this.

Good health is due to the quality of food rather than any special taste or exotic origin. Special dishes of meat and fish may have little nutritional value. Why incur the negative karma of making one's stomach a crematorium when a vegetarian diet suffices? Furthermore, all flesh-and-blood beings are conscious. How shameful it is then to not embrace them as our relatives, much less to kill them and so inspire fear and hatred! By such reasoning one brings forth universal compassion and thus gives up habitual killing.

Through analysis one can also balance temperament. Seeing that all people possess both strengths and weaknesses, one can meet the shortcomings of others with sympathy rather than anger. No one in the world is spotless, thus condemnation is pointless.

What is reasonable about requiring everything of others and nothing of oneself? Mounting daily frustration usually stems from a lack of inner cultivation and discipline. Therefore each person should remain aware of their own thoughts and feelings as these arise.

By regarding any personal provocation as a test of consciousness one will become able to simply acknowledge, rather than to react. In this way one will find that even verbal aggression which "flares throughout the sky" eventually just burns itself out. And yet struggle with every provocation traps the reactive individual as though by a cocoon, when the whole point is to put aside unnecessary conflict.

In summary, then, both killing and anger are self-destructive. The same kind of reasoning applies equally to other psychological and social issues.

Correction at the level of pure awareness: All mistakes [of intention, action, and perception] originate within the basic pure awareness. By abiding in that pure awareness prior to grasping and separative consciousness, one remains free of common errors associated with fame, material resources and sexuality. To lead a pure life requires only determination. Distorted thoughts will then vanish before a virtuous mind just like harmful spirits before the morning sun.

As all faults originate in one's own mind it is there they must be corrected. It is like cutting the harmful tree by its root: this will cause all its branches and leaves to fall off.

Thus the most profound method of correction is at the source of consciousness. Keep your mind purified and remove any unbalanced thought the instant it takes form. If direct awareness is too difficult to practice, then the next best alternative is to regulate one's behavior on the basis of reasoned contemplation. If even this seems too difficult, then one only can correct mistakes as they occur.

It should be clear that mindfulness on all three levels at once is the most effective [because they become mutually supportive]. Merely changing faulty behavior without reasoning and without developing direct awareness is still at the level of working with results rather than causes.

When a person resolves to live the ethical life, it is important to have compatible friends who can provide personal support. It is also necessary to call upon the spirits and divine beings as witnesses. If one makes such a single-minded commitment, and lives this commitment free of interruption, then the result is assured. One may for example feel one's spirit soar, or experience a broadening in consciousness, or remain steadfast in a turbulent situation, or meet enemies with equanimity. The individual may dream of subtle impurity evaporating from the skin in the form of black smoke, or dream of travelling to the stars or to enchanted realms. All these are signs of purification. But one must press on with inner development and not be satisfied with such signs.

As an example, Pa Yu, the sage in Wei Country during the Spring and Autumn Period, had already reflected upon himself and felt that he had corrected all of his mistakes when he was twenty. On reaching twenty-one, he realized the incompleteness of his reflection and rectification. At twenty-two, he looked back and found that his life a year earlier was quite absent-minded, like living in a dream. Year after year, he reflected upon and amended his faults. When he reached fifty, he still found errors committed in previous years. Such is the endeavor of a sage in his inner development.

As common people we are completely burdened with mistakes just as hedgehogs are completely covered with quills. Thus to not see such mistakes simply indicates carelessness and insensitivity.

There are psychological markers associated with strongly negative people: they are commonly disoriented and unable to engage the "here and now". They wring their hands over the smallest matters and feel disconcerted when meeting the virtuous, or when hearing the truth, and even when attempting to assist others, they are only resented. Such people often have chaotic dreams, and they constantly harass others. Thus inner and outer disharmony indicates negative karma. One who recognizes such signs as being characteristic of their own life definitely needs a conscious commitment to inner development and ethical standards to avoid future difficulties.

Essay III. The Ways of Accumulating Merit

3.1 Meritorious Families Have Blessings From Generation to Generation

There once was a Mrs. Yan. When marriage was proposed between her daughter and the father-to-be of Confucius, Mrs. Yan asked only whether the suitor's forbearers had engaged lives of great virtue. She was not primarily concerned whether the family was wealthy because family merit would by itself ensure future good fortune.

Confucius also praised the deep family commitment of a Mr. Shun[1] saying, "Shun will be on the scroll of fame, and his descendants will prosper." This perspective stands to reason, and can be substantiated by the following accounts.

The ancestors of Yang Wing, the Duke of Fujian province, lived as boatmen for generations. Whenever flood rains came, houses were destroyed and the river would sweep away people, domesticated animals, and household valuables. At such times other boatmen hurried only to retrieve the valuables washing down river, while Yang Wing's grandfather saved the drowning people instead. Villagers responded by ridiculing him for "stupidity," but the family prospered over time and had in fact become quite wealthy by the time the Duke's father was born.

One day, a Taoist Master visited the Yang family and said, "Your ancestor humbly accumulated great virtue, hence his descendants are destined to receive wealth and honor. There

---

[1]A legendary Chinese ruler, said to have ruled from 2255-2205 B.C.E.

[2]A term in Chinese geomancy [earth magic] which indicates a place of strong spiritual energy.

is a dragon site[2] in which you should re-bury your ancestor[3]." This was done, and the burial site came to be known as "White Rabbit Tomb." Later Yang Wing was born and even in youth he passed the imperial examination, thus obtaining a prestigious position. Furthermore, his grandfather was posthumously honored by the Emperor, and to this day the family line remains prosperous and a source of many prominent, worthy people.

---

[3] According to Chinese ancestor worship, by burying one's ancestor in an auspicious place, one will receive much benefit from the ancestor's spirit.

3.2 Everyone Can Be Compassionate

In Kan Province, there was once a man called Yang Chi Cheng, who originally worked as a prison guard. He was ethical and compassionate. One day while he was at work, a county magistrate became enraged at a convict and proceeded to whip the man. Mr. Yang felt sympathy for the prisoner and on his knees begged the magistrate for tolerance. The county magistrate responded, "What do you mean, 'tolerance'? This prisoner has committed an atrocity!" Yang bowed and replied, "Because there is so much official mismanagement, people act in desperation and flout the law. This prisoner has already confessed. What more do you want from him?" At this the magistrate calmed down.

Yang Chi Cheng, although born in poverty, never accepted bribery, and he fed hungry prisoners as much as possible, even if this meant going without meals himself. Thus his life was one of continuous charity.

Later he fathered two sons, both of whom became prestigious high-level administrators. Moreover, his first grandson advised the High Court Judge, and the second became Chief Prosecutor in Sichuan Province. Their families prospered greatly, and many of their descendants became government officials.

3.3 Heaven Has Compassion

During the Ming dynasty, civil war broke out in Fujian Province, and many people sided with the rebels. Provincial Governor Hsieh was ordered to suppress the rebellion and eliminate the insurgents. Despite the gravity of the situation, and civilian support of the rebels, Governor Hsieh was determined to minimize bloodshed, and so he employed scouts and informers to identify rebel forces. Before the main government troops arrived to do battle, a government detachment went in. These soldiers secretly distributed small white cloths to neighborhoods and residences which did not belong to the rebels, so that civilians could mark their doors and be spared wholesale destruction.

The governor explained the significance of the white cloths to his forces and forbade them to kill indiscriminately. In this way he saved ten thousand lives. Later, several of his grandsons became government officials of the highest rank and his clan became wealthy.

Also, there once was a Mrs. Lin who lived in the City of Amoy, Fujian Province. In her great generosity she gave bread to the poor each and every day. One monk in particular came by daily to ask for six or seven of the buns. She fed this man for three years without hesitation or complaint. Finally he came to her and spoke as follows: "All this time you have fed me and I have no material means of paying you back. I can however tell you this: spiritual power flows in the land behind your house, and if at death you are interred there, then there will be as many government officials from among your descendants as there are flax seeds in a bottle."

Later, Mrs. Lin passed away and her son followed this counsel. Subsequently, nine of her sons passed the imperial examinations, and in each succeeding generation of this clan there were high government officials. That is why today we have the saying that "There will always be a Lin clan member passing each imperial examination."

Another story concerns the birthright of the chief astronomer and historian, Feng Tso-hang. One winter's day while enroute to school his father-to-be saw a stranger lying in the snow. Mr. Feng removed his coat and wrapped it around the stranger, took him home and began nursing the man back to health.

That night Feng dreamt that a heavenly being approached him and said this: "Because you have saved a man from death, you shall be rewarded with a son who in a previous life was Han Chi, the famous Sung Dynasty general." Mr. Feng did have a most remarkable son, Feng Tso-hang, who later became the imperial astronomer and historian.

3.4 Inner Guidance Inspires Continued Public Service

There once was in Tai Chou Province a State Secretary named Ying. While young he lived in the mountains studying for the imperial examination. Although at night he often heard the noises and talk of disembodied spirits, this did not make him fearful. One night however he paid special attention to a ghost discussing a woman's misfortune. "A Mrs. so-and-so has not heard from her husband since he left home years ago. Now her mother-in-law is forcing her to remarry. She refuses and instead will come here tomorrow night to hang herself. This means that she will take my place in the ghost realm, allowing me to take human rebirth."

Alerted in this way, Ying immediately sold part of his possessions for four ounces of silver, and sent this to the woman's home together with a letter claiming to be from her husband. The mother-in-law received the letter and silver but had great difficulty believing these came from her son. Nevertheless there was no conceivable reason for anyone else to go so far as to send silver, and so the mother-in-law stopped pressing for remarriage. All ended well because the long-gone husband did finally return, and the family joyfully reunited.

Later in the mountains Ying overheard the same spirit's voice one evening, followed by that of another spirit. "That scholar ruined my hopes of exchanging places with the woman." The second voice said, "Then take revenge on him. How will you do it?" The first then replied, "My hands are tied. The Judge of the Dead now personally protects this interloper, and what is worse, this man is slated to become the administrator for our realm. I can do absolutely nothing about it."

This incident had a profoundly life-changing influence on Mr. Ying. From then on he committed himself more and more to public service and increasing his stock of merit. When famine came to the land, he donated grain to directly help those in need. In general he personally helped others with urgent needs, tolerated adversaries and reflected often upon his own shortcomings. The sum total of Secretary Ying's merit was very great, and life responded by blessing him with children and grandchildren who were both wealthy and highly placed. His descendants remain prosperous to this day.

Consider also the life of Hsu Feng-chu, who was born into a wealthy family in Changshu Province. His father personally helped those in need and in particular donated food whenever the community suffered a poor harvest. Eventually Hsu Senior heard a spirit song, which came to him gradually over several days. The song foretold that Hsu Feng-chu would definitely pass the county-level government examination, as in fact occurred later that same year.

As a direct result Hsu Senior further extended his social work, such as commissioning the repair of bridges and roads and aiding travellers and monks. Later his father heard yet another spirit song: "It is true, it is true, Hsu will be promoted to higher office." Subsequently, Hsu Feng-chu became the Inspector of Chekiang Province.

3.5 Freeing Innocent Convicts Brings the Blessing of Heaven

There once was a Mr. Tu Kang-hsi of Chia-hsing Province. When first appointed as Secretary of the Justice Department, he frequently made rounds of the prisons to hear convicts plead their cases. Whenever convinced that a prisoner was in fact innocent, he filed a report to the Chief Prosecutor recommending that the case be reopened. Based on Secretary Tu's reports, more than a dozen convicts were freed.

The Chief Prosecutor won public acclaim for these pardons, while Tu Kang-hsi was content to remain in the background without mentioning his major contribution. Sometime later, Secretary Tu made the following recommendation to the Chief Prosecutor: "Since the Kingdom is so vast and contains so many people, it is quite probable that the prisons contain a significant number of convicts who are in fact innocent. Based on this, I recommend that an investigator be appointed every five years to determine who may be eligible for pardon." The Chief Prosecutor wrote a proposal to the emperor, and obtained approval for creation of such a post. Later Tu became one of the investigators.

Although Tu Kang-hsi and his wife had repeatedly failed to sire children, he later dreamt of a celestial who said that the couple would be blessed with three sons. Soon afterwards, Mrs. Tu did in fact become pregnant, and in the coming years they did raise three sons, all of whom became top government officials.

3.6 Respecting and Protecting the Buddha Way Brings Prosperity

Mr. Pao Ping came from Chia-hsing Province. He was the youngest of seven sons of the town prefect Chih Yang, and a son-in-law to the Yuen family. Despite his intelligence and diligence, he always failed the imperial examinations. Eventually his attention turned to the study of Taoism and Buddhism.

One day, while touring near Tai Lake, he passed by a small village temple, and noticed that the temple roof leaked and the statue of Kuan-Yin Bodhisattva was dirtied by rain. Pao Ping immediately took ten ounces of silver from his pocket as an offering to the senior monk for repairs. The monk said, "To fix the temple roof would take more than this. I am sorry but I cannot fulfill your wishes." Pao then removed every single valuable from his person and gave all to the monk, saying, "As long as the Buddha statue is protected, it is not important whether I have new clothes to wear."

This moved the monk. After a pause, he said, "Donating all one can to the temple is not inherently difficult, but you are doing this from the depth of your heart, which is truly rare." The temple was repaired, and Pao returned for an overnight visit. During the night the guardian spirit of the temple came to him in a dream and thanked him, saying "Your sons will be blessed with high government positions." And indeed his sons Pien and Sheng-fang took high government posts.

There was also a Mr. Chih of Chia-shan province, the father of a Chih Li. While an officer of the court, Chih Senior once encountered an innocent defendant who faced the death penalty. Chih Senior felt sorry for the defendant and wanted to save him. Knowing the good intention of Chih Senior, the defendant had instructed his wife to invite Mr. Chih to their village and to offer herself as a personal servant to Mr. Chih. In tears, his wife promised to do so.

Mr. Chih did in fact come the next day to the village to

visit the defendant's wife, and she expresses that she was willing to serve him if only he would try to help her husband. Mr. Chih refused the offer but promised his best effort on the case. As a result of a large body of evidence, the court found the defendant to be innocent. The man who was tried together with his wife came to thank Mr. Chih for his personal assistance and insisted that their daughter be married to him [as a concubine] to help Mrs. Chih with housework. Mr. Chih could not but follow the custom and accepted. Later, she gave birth a son named Chih Li.

When Mr. Chih's son Chih Li was twenty, the latter passed the imperial examination and became a high official. Furthermore Chih Li's son Chih Kao and his descendants were blessed with wealth.

The anecdotes related in chapters 3.1 through 3.6 differ in terms of application, but all express inner commitment to public service.

3.7 Different Kinds of Virtue

A detailed analysis of virtue shows that virtue takes many forms: authentic and inauthentic, superficial and courageous, open virtue and hidden, long-term and short-term, responsible and complacent, thorough and intermittent, great and small, or difficult and easy. We must consciously differentiate between these or risk mistaking one outcome for another.

It is for example fairly common for people to talk about the lives of others in a rhetorical way. "Mr. so-and-so has been very generous and yet his family life is in pieces. How can this be when other mean-spirited people prosper?" This seeming unfairness causes many to doubt the saying that "*consequences follow as closely as one's own shadow.*"

The basic issue here stems from a fundamental misinterpretation of the nature of virtue. To superficially reject the law of karmic reciprocity is a mistake.

3.8 Authentic and Inauthentic Virtue

Consider what is usually meant by authentic virtue. Rough behavior, miserliness and so forth are considered quite low while politeness, honesty, and personability are deemed worthy. But in fact no actions are intrinsically virtuous or otherwise, because virtue is primarily a matter of the heart and mind. What must be examined is the underlying intention.

Criticizing or even verbally condemning others may be charitable acts if these are intended to benefit others, and respectful courtesy may be merely self-serving. Thus authentic virtue is directed towards furthering others, while inauthentic virtue is directed towards furthering oneself only. Similarly, heart-felt generosity and kindness performed free of ulterior motive are authentic, while ostentatious or calculating acts of "service" are merely inauthentic virtue.

3.9 Superficial and Courageous Virtue

Generally speaking, a prudent, non-contentious individual is upright. However, sages believe that a decisive, quixotic, chivalrous madman can be an upright person. The reason is simple: a quiet individual may be regarded by many as "nice" while merely drifting with the tide. He may carry no aspiration of his own, may not fight for what is right, and possess no courage. There are many such people in this world. Heavenly beings and sages view and judge uprightness quite differently than do common people.

Thus, when we practice charity, we cannot do it just to accommodate social expectations, or to draw the wool over others' eyes. We need to do it from our heart. Helping and caring for others in unexpected ways is courageous virtue.

As for one who practices only a lukewarm form of virtue, that is mere superficial virtue.

3.10 Open and Hidden Virtue

Virtue may also be *open* or *hidden*. Charitable acts known to others are openly virtuous, and are rewarded with prestige and honor from the community. Virtue performed without outward display is rewarded with blessings from Heaven.

One who has more prestige than can be supported by actual virtue will encounter misfortune, as fame and honor are objects of jealousy. Many prestigious people have risen in society due to no merit of their own, thus we see many high-ranked families who encounter one mishap after another. This explains the old saying, "Only fools praise a name lacking substance."

Conversely, someone may be free of misdeeds, yet suffer from scandal and defamation. The individual who can tolerate these without complaint must be a person of substance, and will certainly have descendants who are to be blessed in many ways.

3.11 The Influence of Long-term and Short-term Virtue

Enacting virtue is naturally beneficial both for ourselves and others. What then can it mean to say that there can be both *long-term* and *short-term virtue*? Consider the following historical instance.

In the distant past the minor kingdom of Lu offered large monetary rewards to anyone who would successfully retrieve prisoners of war from a hostile kingdom. A Mr. Tzu-kung had brought back to Lu one such prisoner but refused to accept the reward. Tzu-kung was a student of Confucius, and when the latter learned of this, he scolded Tzu-kung as follows.

"You are wrong. The honorable person's behavior serves as an example and can influence local mores. How can you act in this way without regard for others? The poor people far outnumber the well-to-do in this land and by refusing the reward you have set a bad precedent. In the future others who consider rescue work will have to face embarrassment in accepting the reward that you did not. Thus your action impedes prospective rescue volunteers, and it will be difficult to continue this work."

Another student of Confucius named Tzu-lu also saved a man's life, in this case from drowning. The man's family in their gratitude gave him a cow, which he accepted. Confucius commented that this incident would motivate others to rescue those in danger of drowning.

Most people would consider Tzu-kung's rejection of personal reward to be more virtuous than Tzu-lu's acceptance of a reward, but Confucius took the opposite perspective. This is because the long-term influence of one's attempted virtue must be understood as most important. Instead of viewing individual acts in isolation, their long-term consequences must be considered in advance. The long-term social impact of public service necessarily outweighs short term personal satisfaction.

An individual act of virtue which negatively influences

others must be termed *short-term virtue*, while a seemingly ill-advised act that benefits thousands, is *long-term virtue*. Inappropriate acts include mistaken lenience, fawning flattery that clouds another's capacity for discernment, keeping a minor commitment while allowing a more serious problem to occur, and spoiling one's children. It is therefore necessary to weigh the pros and cons of one's actions in the broader context to determine whether the overall outcome will be positive.

3.12 The Consequences of Responsible and Complacent Virtue

What is meant by *responsible* and *complacent* virtue?

Once there was a former prime minister named Lü Wen-chi who retired to his home village. The local people accorded him great respect, but one day, a drunken local passed by and verbally abused him. Mr. Lü felt that the drunk was temporarily incapable of understanding his own actions and thus did not reprimand the man or call for his arrest.

A year later Mr. Lü was told that this individual had committed a series of crimes which culminated in the latter's state execution. Mr. Lü regretfully commented by saying, "If I had turned him over to the authorities before his offenses became so serious, then court judgements might have taught him to act more responsibly." This illustrates how complacent virtue may lead to negative consequences.

Another example concerns a certain province in a time of famine. Some of the provincials became marauders who robbed others in broad daylight. This caused one established clan to appeal to the authorities but no action was taken. Over a period of some days the marauders became more and more aggressive and the locale extremely unsafe. Finally the clan took the law into their own hands and went after the criminals, breaking a stranglehold of fear on the community.

Thus it is possible to see how complacency can result in serious repercussions while retribution may at times be necessary to safeguard the community.

3.13 Thoroughness of Virtue Depends on Sincerity

What is continuous virtue and what is intermittent virtue? The Book of Changes says, "If one does not continuously accumulate good acts, one will not be deemed charitable. If one does not accumulate negative acts, one won't encounter life threatening disasters." Complete personal dedication is required for continuous virtue, while occasionally good deeds are classed only as intermittent virtue.

There was long ago a poor young woman who visited a Buddhist temple. She had only two pennies to her name yet offered both. As it happened the temple abbot himself performed a purification ritual for her. Years later, the young woman returned as a rich lady, with much gold as an offering, yet the abbot sent a junior to perform the purification rite.

Astonished by this, the lady questioned the judgement of the abbot. "How is it that you once personally helped me for only two pennies, but now ignore me when I offer a thousand gold pieces?" The abbot replied, "With the two pennies you also offered your whole heart, but with all this gold you have only offered a very little from within yourself. Thus the help you receive is in accord with the inner aspect of the offering." Thus in this example, offering a thousand pieces of gold indicates only intermittent virtue, while heartfelt offering of two pennies is thorough virtue.

Long ago the Taoist immortal Chung-li Chuan decided to teach Lü Tung-pin an alchemical method for transmuting iron into gold, to help the poor. Mr. Lü however had doubts about the outcome and asked the immortal whether the magically created gold would ever revert to iron. When told it would after five hundred years, Mr. Lü declined to use this alchemy, saying "Wouldn't you agree that this will seriously harm people when the 'gold' again becomes iron? I do not want to deceive people in such a way, even if the issue is so far removed in time."

Master Chung-li then praised Lü Tung-pin for his sincerity. "To learn the yoga of immortality one must first accumulate at least three thousand good deeds. Your pure intent has just now accomplished all three thousand."

Therefore, charitable work must be performed with a sincere heart. The one who selflessly enacts virtue will accumulate enormous merit even from small deeds, while another who performs a major public service as a means to self-aggrandizement will not accumulate comparable merit.

Consider the action of donating funds without expectation or attachment. With the transpersonal consciousness which perceives donor, gift, and recipient as being one in their essential nature, abide in the *Threefold Open-Dimensionality*, the fundamental level of pure awareness. In this state, giving even one penny generates such enormous merit that the transgressions of even a thousand millennia are erased. And yet offering ten thousand gold pieces with attachment is a lesser virtue.

3.14 The Degree of Merit Depends on Scope of Intent

Virtue can be classed as greater or lesser, as difficult or easy.

There was once a government official named Wei Chung-ta. It happened that in the dream body he visited purgatory, where he was able to examine his life record to date. The book of his life contained only a few pages of good deeds, but many pages of transgressions. The presiding judge asked that the deeds be weighed in a scale, and the numerous pages of bad deeds were outweighed by the few pages of good deeds.

Mr. Wei was deeply puzzled by this, and said, "I have lived only forty years, how could there be recorded so many transgressions?" The judge replied, "Negative thoughts count as offenses, whether or not the individual manifests those thoughts." Wei then asked, "How can my few virtuous actions outweigh so many mistakes?" The judge responded, "The good deeds refer to the appeal letters you wrote to high government officials, asking for stone bridges to make possible a road connecting the three mountains."

Wei said, "I remember the appeals, but what can they have mattered when no action was ever taken?" The judge said, "Although the government did not follow through, the original intention carries tremendous merit because thousands of people would benefit from such a project. If the bridges had in fact been constructed, your merit would be far greater still."

From this it can be seen that the scope of one's intent is of key importance. Focusing on what will benefit the many accumulates great merit, whether or not it is possible to succeed in each attempt. And yet to think only of furthering oneself will on an inner level accomplish little even though outwardly much seems to have been done.

Consider next the distinction between difficult and easy virtues.

Wise elders tell us that inner discipline should be applied where it is most needed. Thus, one should begin to practice more challenging forms of generosity as recounted in the following examples.

In Chiang Hsi province an elderly Mr. Hsu donated two years of his teacher's salary to pay back a loan for a friend, thus allowing the friend's family to reunite.

In Henan province a Mr. Chang paid off with ten years' savings the debt of another man thus saving that man's wife and daughter.

In Chen Chiang province, an old gentleman surnamed Chi preferred to remain heirless rather than wed a young woman.

These charities are most precious because of the selflessness of the individuals, their willingness to undertake what others would not, and endurance of what others could not tolerate. Such virtue will result in great rewards from above.

It is of course more difficult for the poor to enact charity [at least in the outward sense], and yet the commitment to help others, even in unfavorable circumstances, accumulates great merit. Wealthy people of course have far greater opportunities to live in service, but those who choose otherwise abandon the true value of their good fortune.

3.15 Ten Different Ways to Exercise Virtue

Having thoroughly examined the nature of virtue, both outer and inner, the next step is to investigate how to apply oneself in service of others.

Ten categories of service can be identified. These are
1] To encourage people in their performance of virtue.
2] To always keep the sense of respect and loving kindness.
3] To endeavor to assist others in accomplishing their aims.
4] To communicate the importance of benevolence.
5] To respond to others in their time of need.
6] To further projects that will benefit the many.
7] To be generous with material help.
8] To protect and uphold the sacred Buddhist transmissions of wisdom, compassion, and power.
9] To respect one's relations.
10] To open one's heart to all living beings.

1] How does one encourage people in their performance of virtue?

While still young, the emperor-designate Shun of ancient China observed fishermen catching fish in Shantung province. Wherever the fish were plentiful, younger fishermen always dominated, leaving the old and feeble only those areas with poor yields. This deeply upset Shun, so he decided to do some 'socially conscious fishing.' Whenever someone attempted to keep Shun away from a fishing territory, he politely gave way, and conversely whenever others allowed him to fish nearby, he openly thanked them. After some time, respect for others became the norm.

Now consider the fact that Shun was renowned for his

wisdom, and thus totally capable of admonishing others. He nevertheless preferred personal example to command in social situations. How noble and considerate of him!

The point here is that one should not use superior capabilities against others. It is not the purpose of goodness to demonstrate the wickedness of others. Speaking skills are not for chastising others. Respect for all humanity — whether high and low — is necessary, and that universal acceptance includes forgiveness. When someone performs even a minor good deed, then thank them, as a silent protest to the unkind without forcing the latter to lose face. In this way the unkind are gently reminded of the need to reform themselves.

The ideal is to hold uppermost in mind the welfare of others and serve as a role model for universal human values.

2] What does it mean to always keep a sense of respect and loving kindness?

It is not necessarily easy to discern manipulative persons from the pure in heart, and yet by focusing on the priorities which animate a person's activities the difference will be seen to be that between night and day. Thus Mencius said, "The difference between criminals and noble persons is the intention." The sage is one who always engages others in respect and loving kindness.

Consider this traditional saying: "One type of rice feeds a hundred different types of people." People are dissimilar in their development, both outwardly and inwardly. Some are for example wealthy while some are not, and some are intelligent, where others are not. Nevertheless we are all of us brothers and sisters [whether or not this is consciously recognized].

It is therefore essential to extend respect and love to all our fellow human beings from our hearts. Doing so is equivalent to honoring the teachers and healers of mankind, for this is their practice. To learn how to live in this way, to respect others and ourselves equally and thus rest in equanimity is indeed the Way of Heaven.

3] What does it mean to endeavor to assist others in accomplishing their aims?

In the overall social panorama of this world, most people are very lost and confused. Also, people typically tend to protect themselves and exclude others, while those who have the simplicity and directness of heart to help others generally do not know how to flatter and thus are often prevented from obtaining significant opportunity to be of service.

For this reason, those who are well-intentioned should be affirmed and helped. This can be likened to removing the impurities of an unpolished gem, which originally appears like an ordinary stone, but is then revealed to be a treasure.

4] What does it mean to communicate the importance of benevolence?

Every person has a conscience, but this inner sense becomes buried in pretentious and demeaning involvements. People lose themselves to the promises of money and fame. Therefore it is important to gently remind others of benevolence, and what is truly important, to keep matters in proper perspective.

It is said that "A spoken word can educate someone for the moment, while a book can educate the generations to come." If one identifies and engages every opportunity to encourage others in taking up benevolent work, this is comparable to awakening sleeping persons from their nightmares, and thus is a profound form of charity. [One should apply one's wisdom in engaging such an act. Speaking too much may drive away a stubborn person, while being too conservative may lose valuable opportunities.]

5] What does it mean to respond to others in their time of need?

All of us face critical challenges and turning points in

our lives. Thus we should empathize with others in their times of need, just as if we faced comparable situations. We can always comfort others with kind words, remain available to their pain, or provide help in other ways. As it is said, "Personal support need not be something very involved, just be available when called upon."

6] What does it mean to further projects that will benefit the many?

This refers to social welfare, developing and participating in activities that benefit the general public, such as irrigation systems, bridges, or economic assistance programs. One may contribute either time or money to such programs.

7] What does it mean to be generous with material help ?

Generosity is the first and most important virtue among the Great Way Buddhist precepts. The bodhisattva [spiritually evolved person] can give to others whatever he or she possesses, including outer and inner capabilities. This is because such a person is unattached to the five senses.

Since common people cannot be expected to follow such an example, they can instead begin by giving money to charities. Common people can be characterized in large measure as those who regard money as more important than life and death, and thus for them few situations are as disagreeable as having to part with money. Therefore financial generosity not only serves to benefit others and increase meritorious power, it can also free one's awareness from grasping at the provisional self. Such generosity greatly furthers inner cultivation.

Such an approach may initially be accompanied by inner reluctance but will progressively bring about inner peace and the purification of one's cognitive and conative errors.

8] What does it mean to protect and uphold the sa-

cred transmission of wisdom, compassion, and power?

The Buddhist Discipline is a sacred transmission which nurtures inner nobility in people. Without this type of transmission, the world would utterly lack the light of intelligence and spiritual evolution. What means would there be for living beings caught in cyclic existence to free their true natures? One should therefore revere the precious Buddhist places and scriptures, and disseminate the Discipline of Awareness, thus repaying the compassion of the Awakened Ones.

9] What does it mean to respect one's relations?

This means to be considerate and accommodating of family members, teachers, and elders in society. One should speak in a balanced and moderate way with parents, and comply with the laws of the land. When given significant authority, one should perform the assigned duties without conceit or arrogance. All of these are classified as hidden virtue.

10] What does it mean to open one's heart to all living beings?

An ancient homily says, "If you love the rats, leave them some scraps of food; if you pity the moths, do not light the lamp." Of course it is very difficult for the majority of people to embody such kindness, but the homily does remind us of the importance of compassion. Mencius observed that "the wise stay away from the kitchen."

While many individuals find the vegetarian diet restrictive, it is certainly practical to abide by the Buddhist forbearances concerning meat, which are to not raise animals to be slaughtered, to not ask that an animal be killed for our meal, and to not accept as food an animal that has been killed for oneself. It is important to avoid satisfying ourselves through the suffering of others, and, instead, to bring forth compassion and intuitive discernment.

Furthermore, even clothing ourselves can involve the death of many living beings, as when many silkworm cocoons are boiled to obtain the silk covering the chrysalis. Thus, one should make good and economical use of all that one has, and avoid unnecessary killing.

In summary, there are many avenues by which to exercise virtue. One can start with the ten listed herein and progressively realize the spirit of service.

Essay IV. Humility

4.1 The Value of Humility

The Book of Changes says, "The way of Heaven disperses the full[1] and raises the lowly. The way of earth changes the full and spreads humility. Spirits injure the full and bless the humble. The way of humans is to dislike the full and prefer the meek."

There are sixty-four hexagrams in the Book of Changes, and each hexagram is associated with six [basic] variations with their commentaries. Two-thirds of the three hundred eighty four variations are unfavorable, and yet all six variations for the hexagram "Humility" are highly auspicious. This explains the old saying that *one loses through arrogance and gains through patience.*

There are many examples of poor and humble individuals who achieved riches and success.

One year I recall that ten men from my village journeyed to Peking to take the Imperial Examination. Among them was Ting Pin, who was the youngest, and the most humble and polite as well. I told a friend that Ting Pin would pass that Examination, and he asked why.

I responded, "Only the modest and subdued can truly be blessed. Look around this group — only Ting Pin is really trustworthy and subdued. He patiently endures slander and refuses to dispute with people. Anyone this mature would have to receive supernatural help. How can he not pass the exam?" That year Ting Pin did in fact pass the examination.

There are other examples, such as County Administrator Fang of Che Chiang Province, Mr. Chao of Shantung, and Mr. Hsia. Each repeatedly failed the Imperial Examination. And yet each was able, after correcting haughty and conceited behavior, to pass the examination.

When Heaven bestows grace on someone, the transfor-

---

[1]Here "full" refers to pride and arrogance.

mation begins with opening up that person's awareness. Once a person has profound insight, he or she will put aside negative behaviors and what we call "good fortune" will follow.

In Che Chiang province lived a very intelligent man named Mr. Chang. He was famous for his high scholarship, but in 1594 he took the Imperial Examination and failed. Infuriated, Chang began to verbally abuse the examiner. As it happened, there was a Taoist nearby who began to smile, and noticing this, Chang turned to attack this Taoist instead.

The Taoist said, "Perhaps your essay was not good enough!", and Chang furiously replied, "You haven't read it, so how could you know?" The Taoist then responded "I have heard that only a clear-minded person can write a good composition. Seeing you act so impulsively makes me wonder how you could possibly write a good essay."

Chang was humbled by this, and asked the Taoist for guidance. The latter replied, "Passing the exam depends significantly on one's personal level of evolution. If your inner development has not yet reached the necessary level, then what is necessary is for you to change yourself." Chang asked, "But isn't this a matter of fate, and if so, how can one alter it?"

The Taoist responded, "On one level, one does begin life with a certain level of development, and if a person does not seek to definitely develop themselves, then that is what is called 'fate'. However, the individual who sets out to live a life of virtue, who decides for example to always be charitable towards others, will eventually become able to accomplish anything whatsoever."

Chang said, "I have no resources, so how can I possibly give to others?" The Taoist said, "Charity springs from the heart. If you can always keep your heart open towards others, then each outward action will reflect that and bring benefit. For example, you need not spend money to be humble. In the present situation, you should reflect upon your own shortcomings rather than blaming the examiner. Ask yourself what you can do to purify and strengthen your consciousness so that in the next exam you can succeed."

After that, Chang started to practice charity daily. One night, he dreamt that he entered a building and picked up a Book of Records. Many names had been erased from this book, and so he asked someone standing nearby what the book represented. The man replied, "This is a list of people who are supposed to pass the exam this year." Chang then asked, "Why are so many names erased?"

The man replied, "Every three years we in the nether world reassess the list of those persons who are supposed to pass the Imperial Examination. Only those who have refrained from negative acts and who have accumulated significant merit remain on the list. The names erased are those who have committed serious errors." The man then indicated an entry in the Record Book and said, "These last three years you have been very careful in your behavior. It is therefore likely that you can pass this exam with this ranking." Indeed, Chang passed the examination, ranking 105th.

Thus there is real truth in the old saying: "Never do wrong. Three feet above one's head stand the divine beings." We live in a world filled with misfortune, and the only truly effective way to avoid misfortune is to keep one's heart and mind pure. If one can have a warm and loving heart, and respect for nature and the supernatural beings, and remain cautious, then one will be guided and cared for by the invisible forces.

However, a life of vanity and pride, or careless execution of responsibilities, will inevitably lead to a dark and uncertain future. In that case, what good fortune one may have will not endure. Thus the wise will not cut themselves off from goodness by arrogance and contempt. It is through receptivity that one can receive guidance from others, and this in turn makes possible inner purification and development. Thus such an attitude is necessary for those who wish to practice the inner disciplines.

Part of a Buddhist prayer says that with the practice of inner purification "... one who asks for riches, shall have riches, and one who asks for fame shall obtain it." Heaven will definitely respond to one who remains humble and allows others to live their own lives. Therefore, success is a matter of the purity of one's own attitude.

Mencius said that, "One who takes up the ethical way of life and decides to live for the benefit of all people shall realize inner peace and eternal joy." Most people however look only to their own immediate future, and lack the long-term determination necessary for success. Being short-sighted, they lack persistence.

It is therefore clear that those who want to change their lives require both a definite goal and real determination, and the accumulated merit of many charitable acts to carry their intention forward.

Books available from Purple Lotus Society:

The Inner World of the Lake
by Grand Master Sheng-yen Lu

    In this book, Grand Master Lu weaves the insights he has at the edge of Lake Sammamish (in Washington State) with his episodes of seeing Dakinis above the lake, saving water spirits, and reading messages on the mirror of the lake. The lake is no longer an ordinary body of water in Grand Master Lu's sight but is transformed into the Lake of Self Nature (Buddha Nature). Sharing his thoughts, feelings, and happenings at the edge of the lake, in simple but graceful language, the reader can easily glimpse into the mind of this enlightened sage, and comprehend the esoteric wisdom of Tantric Buddhism. The appendices provide valuable teachings on some of the basics of Tantric Buddhist practices.

$13.95 retail

Mystical Experiences of the True Buddha Disciples
by Grand Master Sheng-yen Lu

    Through the practice of Tantric Buddhism, an individual can develop his/her spiritual energy to a degree that many wondrous events will occur around him or her. Such happenings are not just reserved for the advanced practitioner but also occur to the initiate through the power of one's teacher. This book chronicles the many remarkable things that have happened to students of Grand Master Lu such as clairaudience, mystical phenomena in meditation, a Buddha appearing in the sky, foretelling dreams, remission of serious illnesses and much more.

$10.00 retail

A Complete and Detailed Exposition on the True Buddha Tantric Dharma
by Grand Master Sheng-yen Lu

    The nuances and subtleties required for successful Tantric Buddhist practice are meticulously laid out by Grand Master Lu in a special discourse given at the Rainbow Villa in western Washington in 1992. Grand Master Lu, in this discourse, shares the wealth of

information he has obtained from his twenty spiritual masters so that practitioners can quickly attain spiritual response from their Personal Deity. Showing the various visualizations, mantras, hand gestures, and breathing techniques necessary for a highly effective practice, Grand Master Lu enables the practitioner to quickly progress towards Buddhahood. The reader can learn the methods for invoking deities, paying homage to the deities, guarding against negative forces, merging consciousness with one's Personal Deity, and entering into samadhi.
$10.00 retail

Encounters with the World of Spirits
by Grand Master Sheng-yen Lu

Grand Master Lu's unique spiritual odyssey began one day in 1969. While disinterestedly watching a Buddhist Festival, Grand Master Lu was called out from the crowd by a trance medium and told the Buddhas wanted him to spread the Dharma. That night, Grand Master Lu was magically transported to the magnificent Buddha realm known as the Maha Twin Lotus Ponds and greeted by many Bodhisattvas. During the next several years many remarkable and mysterious happenings transformed Grand Master Lu's life. An invisible teacher from the spiritual realm came to teach Grand Master Lu various esoteric arts and an old Taoist teacher in the Taiwan Mountains taught Grand Master Lu ancient Taoist techniques. In the meantime, Grand Master Lu exorcised spirits from the spiritually possessed, assisted various departed spirits, and spoke with various heavenly beings. This book will inspire anyone oriented towards the esoteric arts.
$10.00 retail

Dharma Talks by a Living Buddha
by Grand Master Sheng-yen Lu

From Dragon Kings to Buddhahood, Grand Master Sheng-yen Lu covers the gamut of esoteric subjects in his many Dharma talks. Recognized as a Living Buddha by many Tibetan Tulkus including Kalu Rinpoche, Grand Master Lu brings a unique perspective to the Buddha-dharma. Making arcane subjects easily accessible, Grand Master Lu opens the Inner Way to all people. This book is tremendously rich in teachings, including the invocation of the Six Wealth

Deities, the method of inner cultivation, purification of meat, and guidance for entering the Buddha Pure Lands.
$10.00 retail

Pamphlets available from Purple Lotus Society:

1.1 Mystical Experiences
1.2 Sariras—Executed Prisoners Achieve Buddhahood
1.3 Manifestation of the Purple Lotus
1.4 Expanding One's Consciousness
1.5 How to Quiet the Mind
1.6 How to Set Up a Tantric Shrine
1.7 Realization of a Spiritual Master (Book Excerpts)
1.8 Striking Power of Zen (Book Excerpts)
1.9 Brief Repentance Yoga (A Preliminary Practice)
1.10 Vajrasattva Yoga (A Preliminary Practice)
1.11 Mantras and Sutras to Remove Negative Karma
1.12 Questions and Answers on the True Buddha School
1.13 Tibetan Tulkus and Living Buddha Lian-Sheng

The pamphlets are free although donations are welcome to cover printing and shipping costs.

For all orders, please include the following shipping and handling charges:

Please include $2.00 shipping for 1st book and $1.00 for each additional book. Outside the United States, please include $3.00 for 1st book and $1.50 for each additional book. All payments must be in US currency. California residents please add 8.5% sales tax.

To order, please send order and payment to:
Purple Lotus Society, Publishing Department
627 San Mateo Ave.
San Bruno, CA 94066
Fax:(415) 588-1785

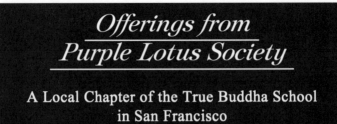

Offerings from
Purple Lotus Society

A Local Chapter of the True Buddha School
in San Francisco

Free Subscription
Purple Lotus Journal

The Purple Lotus Society has a free bilingual Journal for anyone with an interest in Buddhism or Taoism. Articles and speeches by Grand Master Lu concerning Vajrayana, Chan (Zen) Buddhism, Pure Land Buddhism, and Taoism are featured in the Journal.

Group Meditation

The Purple Lotus Society holds meditation every day at 7:00 am and 7:30 pm. On Tuesday nights when Master Samantha Chou is in town, a Bardo Ceremony is held.

Spiritual Assistance

Master Samantha Chou, a manifestation of the Purple Lotus Bodhisattva, uses her spiritual power to help individuals every Tuesday and Saturday afternoons. Please call for an appointment.

Purple Lotus Society

636 San Mateo Ave.
San Bruno, CA 94066
(415) 952-9513